AF752251

THE DECADENT MOVEMENT

PITT POETRY SERIES

Nancy Krygowski and Jeffrey McDaniel, *Editors*

The Decadent Movement

Laura Kolbe

Poems

Published by the University of Pittsburgh Press, Pittsburgh, Pa., 15260
Copyright © 2026, Laura Kolbe
All rights reserved
Manufactured in the United States of America
Printed on acid-free paper
10 9 8 7 6 5 4 3 2 1

ISBN 13: 978-0-8229-6836-8
ISBN 10: 0-8229-6836-3

Cover art: Sabine Lepsius, *Self-Portrait* (*Selbstbildnis*), 1885. Oil on canvas, 25 x 32.9 in. Nationalgalerie, Staatliche Museen zu Berlin.

Cover design and book design by Alex Wolfe

Publisher: University of Pittsburgh Press, 7500 Thomas Blvd., 4th floor, Pittsburgh, PA 15260, United States, www.upittpress.org

EU Authorized Representative: Easy Access System Europe, Mustamäe tee 50, 10621 Tallinn, Estonia, gpsr.requests@easproject.com

for Sandro

⊙

coauthor of some months

of those practices the stepping out into love, motion's
glimpse, blanches to the highest burn: I can lose myself:

—A. R. AMMONS, "Hibernaculum"

CONTENTS

⊙

AFTERWORD

January

What was this year—a long fear stretched
till it broke like taffy and caught itself up?

A bowl where dripped the blood I ushered
from myself, afraid that if I didn't take it

out of me and store my life in secret,
it would be robbed so cunningly I'd forget

I'd once loved din, disorder, all the box
Pandora's minders say we must lament.

I worried being smoothed down till I couldn't
know myself. That those lead aprons—pregnant,

parent—would halt the rays of light
and danger that pierced me to the bone,

frizzed my genes in ways I'd come
to love, a life distressed and broken-in

and comfortably unkempt. I kept
a diary in poems the moment I knew

an embryo attached inside me. Dreamed
I'd publish all in sequence—Muybridged

out so anyone could see, framed, a woman
running for her life, angry and afraid

of change even though I'd chosen
and kept choosing to go on. I wanted:

Progeny without supplanting. Experience
without the marks of age or pause.

Grace without conversion. *That* book
would show how staunch I'd hugged

my dry cocoon. How much it meant
to me to die in life as I knew it, how

even as I pushed a baby, some stash of
me refused. Instead when I read backward

I better saw a span of life ranged with newish
mountains, faces sheared here and there

to room more lift, and not to smooth or numb.

THREE AND A DOG

January

We clack the mini farmer back in the toy barn.
The roof hinges on sleeping sheep.
For dinner viscosities now there's three:

One for eight teeth, one for fifty-six
(Two adults, their wisdoms gone),
One for old canines, wet and cigarette-tan

At the base, that chew what they might
And not what they can. The farmer's a man
With a big bandanna, not a bad stand-in

For A., his notebooks specked
Like quail eggs and laid on the table
In broods, closed in, spooled up, the yeoman

Checking his chicks and commas before
The night. Peanut butter on German
Many-grained brown bread: S. strains

Peanut kernels off the top and chews
What's smooth: not much: a flush of apricot
Jam and all the rest splayed down his tongue

In four dark shingles. I hope the milk
Makes up for the rest. B. eats beets
And frittata off the floor. On hard days

I am the roof to the farmyard barn, I feel:
Bright-turning on thin brass, then fog-
Colored planks of me spread

In a washed wood extent. Gray paint standing
In for slate. A chill acoustic cover. An echo
Membrane snapping at clefs as clams eat,

Letting the sand gem the walls
Colorless, nacred. Necessity the mother.
I am the roof of my mouth

And more: meshed complex of various
Hardbound moistures whose synching concert,
Fires and contractions, writ sixty-four inches large,

Wins bread. How strange. How hinged on organs
Clacking along, on thought's mostly-lost
Steam, and this is how the barn stays raised?

Am I also the sparrow through the atrium—
It's a makeshift hall now, this barn,
It's like a hospital, this too-clean machine,

What Saint Bede said about the squeaking
Brevity of passage between one cracked window—
Life—as though a bird swooped in, and faster out,

The musk of wild vanishing behind it
On the cleaning-fluid updraft as the hall's
Wiped down. How strange, how flanged

Along the toy barn's sturdy gambrels,
Its imaginary gutter-line where invisible birds
Shunt ice-cream-cone-shaped homes

From which to catch flies atop the wooden horse,
My thinking of my death, right here.
My earnings then my death. But three,

We're three, we're three and a dog, and being
Tethered in triangle, strongest—supposedly—
Shape aids the false feeling of being permanently

Here. I'll take it! So much to bewitch
Just now: at bathtime I admire on S.
The dollops of deltoids and biceps, sleepy

Ladyfingers, soaked and lolling like hatched turtles
Stunned by the sea. *And they lived in a warm*
Wooden tree, Brown's perfect story goes,

And how we do, apartment ardent, towels and emotions
Porous as toast. Dry off, pat the near-black curls
So they snap up again like crickets

Or mousetraps, crisp and busy, piercing me, love,
it's almost too much. Good night, I ache,
Good night. S. clucks and sinks. In the barn

Of the farmer the farmer seldom rakes
The straw beneath the sheep, it's not
A fun game, it's not Peekaboo or Celebrity

Or Huckle Buckle Beanstalk, it's not anything,
Putting toys away or cleaning the clothes,
But a colossal theft of someone's time. Mine?

Or yours? We bicker on this point and swindle
More from each other, expensive minutes that could
Have bought another line in A.'s novel

Or in this poem. Fifty-six teeth: that's four
Operatic rows, a Family Circle catching
The augmented triad and the gleaming

Rests, the supertitles jack-o'-lanterned so we know
Just what each keening means. I've turned
Mine off, sometimes, when A. bel cantos—

Opted not to read what I wish not
To know. I do not want, sometimes,
His burning tower. Mine's enough,

This stage. Then the mezzanine cocktail:
Remorse, love, and etiquette, up straight,
Well drink, all's well. I remember when

I read and wrote all day on the craigslist table,
Bag of granola and jar of water at my elbow, window
Cracked for the lilac and the neighbor-dog's nails

Glittering the vinyl patio. "Snout" would be his name
In supertitles, the actual a cabriole I couldn't
Execute. His owner trilled it Iberian

About the yard. Nothing stopped me, those days,
In my novel (an Italian medical student,
Homesick, corn-dazed in Pennsylvania,

Entangled in two men) except its cureless badness
And the odd shower. So happy! Writing badly
So much every day! So much remembered

About one's twenties is still here, a bit smaller
Or paler, shirts shrunk too hot, the books
Whose ramparts have been egged by the sun.

I wear everything that's happened to me
And some things that haven't but expropriate
Beautifully in accordion pleats. Dress-up's a sport

I forget I love to play until I'm there. So what
If I don't for lack of time write of all that
Interests me or makes me yearn, velvet adornments,

Adorno, Duccio, Goya, grammar, The Haitian
Revolution, the Bayeux tapestry, Guatemalan huipils,
Henry James, incense perfumes, public radio

At sunrise in a cold car (those hopeful old
All Things Considered horns!), cowboy shirts,
Schubert, Bert and Ernie and Sesame Street,

Maurice Sendak, Edward Said, how he-said-she-said
Works on a formal level in hospitals, novels, opera, and therapy,
It's not a race, this kind of need is more like a bee's

If I'm being honest, it's programmed, in theory
All the flowers, please, but de facto I'll just dunk
My head wherever, come up covered in floral

Pistil shots. I won't do everything I want—so what?
That birds spin just for bugs is no less lovely
Of them. The object can be dull and small,

I'll eat bugs too, soon, I don't mind as long
As it's a mashed patty and spicy and everyone's
Doing it, it'll probably save a delicate crust

Of the planet from overroasting. Will I be more
Generous when there's less to go around?
I wouldn't mind a life all secondhand of touched

And weathered castoffs—have mostly built
Books and wardrobe so—we rent—I like a lover
Whose last encounter's evident—

I like to be late to a scene picked over,
Awaiting revival—I like eating the food
S.'s left behind, I've even eaten what

He's spit right out, as long as barely chewed
Or wet, it's grace, it's like alms, and tastes
No different than if he'd only held that cube

Of mango in his palm. I've a weird fear
Of wasting, but even more I like to stretch
This epoch of two bodies being one. It's last call,

Past time to be done, I've pulled this
S./Mama symbiosis phase beyond all
Acceptable shape, like yanking sheer tights

Over one's head to rob a counter. (The scariest
Thing I saw in the paper when I was six—
The eyes matte shoe-soles, face like a skull.)

Two and a dog awake, this Sophie Calle
/Greg Shephard movie makes me sad couples
Never hear each other's thoughts in time

To change. Even two people in a car preferred
To tell the camera of a mood, and not breathe
An audible alm to the other till later

They edited the tapes. A. takes B. out to pee,
I roll up the moribund toothpaste tube to get what's left,
Past natural shape it's a telescope, it's a diploma,

Noble ring through which the long view
Leaks an astral applause. Habit's cowlick's
Big as the Milky Way. In bed our two quilts start

Mille-feuille style atop each other, a printed draft,
But drift apart until we're incubated separate
As buns. I open A.'s, or he does mine,

In the moment it seems crucial who moves first
Though never after remembered, each in
Our separate disaster of intended thought

He or she didn't think much less transcribe today,
Prickly and sour from that, feeling owed,
Feeling tired and tared back to zero, this cranky friction

Flips, perhaps, the drydocked hull in which we berth
As family, makes us snarled strangers, with all
The injury and wonder a stranger can arouse.

Thank God. This fold, this bowl, this cupola: these parts
I pick up until they become one unit of intention:
I do not know who all this belongs to while

It's happening. Later we're tired and relieved
And soft with new skin: the tingle of taking
Off braces or a cast. Quilts on again, one handmade

Hand-me-down from someone else's wedding,
The other mass-made paisley from our generation's
Most liberal big box. Two weights shedding

Thread while we sleep, to the floor, the air—
Everything winds up everywhere, that's thermodynamics,
That's a family reaping its subsistent furrow

While another family gleans behind it.
At dawn S. will stand in his crib like a farmer
At the plough, egging on the next turn

Of the whipped world, but now we are four lumps
Still and apart, vinegar-poached for the bite
That fixes us solid, soft, each exhaling

Sheeted dome a planetarium, a view of the light.

TEACHING SPEECH

December

Saying yes to no and yes to yes to
the baby boy so many times a day
it's like a people's protest chant gone non-
electric harboring a claim belonged
to everyone who cares, we care, we crawl
outside and spy more life to point and yes
at with a name. What do you call the fence
around a tree? Who is the life you seek
when indexing the noon moon's matte navel,
gray and nervous, and tell her wait for night?
To mother is a power ever to be
repeating, peat-cut to provide a weight
of burnable goods by eons replaced,
a turf, a moniker, another yes.

FILM MAUDIT

October

When the baby is asleep I leave
Home a few seconds take
The dog and pace the edifice.

Her burning gold ellipses excuse mine
All over the plants. You at the movies watch

A city, a season, a shadow hand
Its keys to anyone who wants to live
With a picture: *Here, would you like*

To join us in Paris?
To enter unannounced? You are our boyfriend
Now. We love you—we the lead

And all the extras. Life is very bright
Screened before you. An x-ray all bone
Unbroken, airless, splitless, a Shirley

Temple umbrella bigger, more important than
Drink itself, which is sweet and in this schema
Cups life's fundament, the molecules we call

Wet when polar charge holds them just
A little, not too much, a cuddle with a cutoff
Granting spillage and expanse. The rustle—

Pacified phone somewhere, beer clicking inside
Purse a row behind you—is the music
Of the dangle of those keys to life afloat

Above your grasp. Their brass teeth form
The plumage flashed in that long mating

Dance with doors. The two kinds
Of movies and marriage are hinges
And hasps. And you are in a double

Feature—your neighbor shakes
A popcorn bag, Anna Karina tosses
Her hair, everything twinkling and rattling

Those exit keys again. . . . You could have closed
Your palm around their cool. Unlocked
A celluloid self gullivered with just

Your face, but out of this world's zip
Ties and stake-downs, the cobwebby ropelets,

Any one trivial—but so many! and together salient
As picnic ants—this other you now sails
On swift to his next world and time.

The two kinds of movies and marriages are:
The outbound and the inbound—

Whether, steering ship,
On your right is starboard or
The port—the hero coming home, convening—

Whether there is a port to speak of.
My kind of line is to be sequined
Here, a simple stitch, lilliputian

But cumulative, a mermaid mail
That makes all the little saucers shine
Just by holding on to some kind

Of backcloth while the torso
Moves in the light. Sequins: that's my kind
Of motion: fixed and also beam-shook,

Tilt-mad, tailored on the bias, and photographs
Well. Here I stay, but feral yet. Anchored
But crazed, tied at the mast without my cotton.

Your kind might be something more
Shorn, less shine, more free.
Not that you would do anything

But stay. This marks the difference, though—
Your good will and its long and notional leash—
My needle through the eye

Of the sequin of me. My shining
With adherence. There are how many
Kinds of necessity, and how do we know

We attach to what we love exactly right?
Dog and I are done with burning out
A track for ourselves between the trees

And further go into the nylon-dark block
Feeling it pill where overtouched.
We'll go back to the baby in a moment in

His crib in the tightest tailoring
He will ever know, smother proof, the low
Couture of need sewn onto need—

But it looks good in the projector
Room I carry in a velvet
Jewelbox in my skull.

It looks like we are all safe and here, breathing.
Here on the block it's the live world still.
A man rolls by with a red wire cart

Full of cans to loosen the deposits from
The state into his palm. The night's
A good time to collect. A nickel apiece.

A stepped-on one's a ringer
For a shining cervix,
Its tabbed mouth leaking

Tart sugar water or grain
Gone off. Or saucer of a lens cap,
Keeping looking safe, keeping the moving

Picture-maker uncracked even
In the listing roll of every shot scene of
Every voyage out and back.

IN FLOWER

August

Too straight for those we also love to find
spare keys to open us, too unsparing,
unspared, to stay as we are, e.g., last
week, gay beach, peach cloud of women topless,
their hands in each other's hair like puppies
tossing salad, we two a gull's-length from
that primrose nebula of friends, we played
the Man-With-Woman, Woman-With-Her-Man
game, fat baby between us, you watched me
hear the Call of the Wild, you saw my hair
stand up at the neck as though a breeze . . . yes I've
been Balbec'd before, but this was the miss-
ion I'd hold like a hot beach ball where my
fingerpads are thick enough to stand it.

WRITING AND NURSING

August

I began to see writing and nursing as one
looped process whereby expressing caused the body
to widen and deepen its reserves, to beef up to
the point of pain—the point of ugliness—

small marbles under the skin like tumors
or ladybugs, dots upon dots, parasites
begging to be pushed out to the world's
relief through stress of one other person wanting
what was inside, the white jet—or even
without that person, the stream

could continue months or years with the right
machine, something that mimics a baby
and the hard chain-link shape of the baby mouth,
something that pulls fast first then lazy
but stronger, like what Marcella Hazan said
of Italian cooking and Madhur Jaffrey of Indian,
that you start with a cruel and "lively heat"
under the tomatoes to bring them
to heel but very briefly then simmer
in butter for ages with almost no force. Hungry,

now, writing this, I know that hunger
is countersigned by my breasts—imagine
a nipple dipped in ink, a contract
where the enemy of my enemy is
one theory of movement
of a blotted politics—this appetite squashes
what it needs to, blackens and redacts
thought and project to make more milk,

to make more fat in me so the milk
can be rich later, even if I stopped
everything—eating, pleasure, even
if a lively heat held off crops—in the short term
fat milk would stammer on.

The *soffritto*—first step of many national
cuisines, from sub + frying, not suffering,
though my ear is tin and prying
the peels apart, prefix from root, harder
than crushing garlic or grammar skin
and all—that's the term for higher heat
untampered by water or excess juice.
Now you're really cooking, when you
can resist the urge toward an ending and enter
the components one by one, often

from driest to finally the kinds of leaves that carry
in stiff stalks their own power to cloud,
to make it rain inside a lidded dish—

but what exactly hurts
is the "let-down," sometimes, midwife-speak
for milk when first released after curling
in its bulbs and trails inside
the breast deciding the tension is
unbearable so there must—the breast
with its slow, generic thoughts thinks—be
a creature outside, there must
be guest, there must, come out!, be someone
to feed to explain why I feel so. A bit

like the start of a "writing day," some idiot's term,
what to call it when the business is only
to be pumped, to express, and after get yourself
straight, cordoned, pared and cored—but early
on you will lack even these labors because
one must first ooze out a thick expression

of letters, balled up suspended
particles like fat in milk.
Milk has ruled me as writing
has ruled me, in squat shudders
of pain with no proportion
to output, which can for all the buildup be a pinched
crude approximation of real storms like the shot blue dribbles
of wiper fluid from a car—the way forward
screened by colloids of upflung organics
on glass, gray porridge of dead arthropods
(from "jointed feet," like a poem) that nobody loved
but persist far longer than their brief lives
across the miles and the shield—just so the milk
that I express is sometimes more
and sometimes less than what I would have guessed

from bare hazard. I am hot, sub-frying
in my house robe and a greasy chore—
the milk, the line—becomes more massy
and opaque each minute I think
about it, more than weather-haze,
than cumulonimbus or the tempered pane

of glass, the shield within which all drive,
the miles from home, the writing
and the nursing forming rather a person
out of nearly-nothing, out of bone leach and election
to pull and be pulled, allowing this
to happen to the body and the brain,
the milk and the line advancing, creeping, longer than
the first straits ever cut a defile in the land and long
past when the backflown slurry of
the earth must go on righting it.

PLAYOFFS

June

Reading Arendt-McCarthy letters
in bed with the NBA
seeping under the door.
The game's become
too strong's a way
the old say there's no
thought in speed.
That gifts should be
allocable, forensic
as tracked packages, lest
mystery proceed.
My friends have lightning
gifts and dodge
the world. And also crumpled
slowness sweet to see.
To me few write singly.
Life's bulked up.
We all talk in hoops.
It's night: azaleas,
witty, bloody, barely
hold on then
barely drop
their blooms.
Whate'er they do's
like doing nothing

best. Hey, look:
there's rabbits underneath.
Like blood moons:
larger seen
through trees.
And leeched and lit
by the bona fide
moon, minnowish
oak leaves, sterling,
darling, flash
their rapid costly
grants. I've nothing
to contribute but
my matterhorn subject,
my every last
and red ascent.

FIRST CUT

on trimming S.'s hair
June

did I make that
(him) or what if I hadn't been
before
the maker but now capable was
making it stick?   maybe very
stuck, had been, he, pro tem

a life refulging
too changing every
day to speak of it (didn't)
and I cut his hair today like
slicing
an orange or netting
a Christmas tree did I
reckon the resin

of a ringed feeling
stacked on
my fingers
in this grave kisslike experience
how did I pile him

aside from himself
        strange   before bed
as he slept, after, did I   yes
        samples in envelopes

I will send those chestnuts to the moon!

would hang
        these victorianas   secular novenas
tralalas
for cable news

        (and to   his grandmothers don't
have the same sweet
        teeth for locks

        but mail has many converts, see
        Titus, Romans, Timothy
)

MARCH 25, 2023

Cold wind through the market again.
Coats out from under the bed,
their brief unhappy resurrection—
those worn folks in paintings carrying
their hides at final trumpet.

Your black wool, its bottle-green lining
shredding old lettuce, my puffer
shiny at the elbows.

Some things seem to obey
the alphabet today. Wind whips.
Robins redoubt. Afternoon's
brave cooks don ear-flap gusset hats—
it's just kale, last month's, nubucked over.
Persisting, quiet, rough.

Quite enough!
The world tardy this year, and still
too fast . . . I am, for example, thirty-six.
With age the human lens denatures
and the full blaze of world's white gets lost
from what we see. Not yet, I think,
for me: the plastic tip jars
from pretzel and pickle barrels
still give one of white's varieties:
the dog-eyed kind that rolls and stains.

Another white from the butcher
twine light that holds itself
and a few select muscles on a pan
of ground, lets the day's oils
slide in slats. And big scones of cloud, a pill-pale
white sliced yellow at the center traced
with Jersey sulfur.

Let us defer
to astronomical spring, here and five days
old, however slipped with tired
and frozen things, and come out
with our babies and forsythia lambed
and then felined with half-frosted feet.
And under our coats keep
no layers we could not as easily
remove. A spring *we,* a local *we,*
smudged by the fan of clayish washout
on the park path. And so long
as we keep finding whatever little-brown-job
birds stir up our cerebral glossary
and incite a pen in the chore coat,
pecking at the dropped shoppings
as they do, the metronome of Saturdays
will stretch out its neck like a horse
for us from grain to lippy grain.

The fat, smooth park in March
and the pocked, wee market:
like a ring resized down
and its comma of refunded tact.
Like any insistence on snug fit,
it wagers on the future as commodity
with some sap still, the truth. Just so
the park begins early on its angles
and dewpoints, cranking Avogadro's number
for finding pale atoms in so much of mostly
just space. It's cold, devices say.

Let us submit
that this was the week's end, but also
the beginning of the next. I'll take
the baby now, bale him in blankets
and sift the stalls for last apples
that still pepper the nose in
starry lemon tones. You go home
and sleep. We're at a pale point
where distance from each other feels
like kindness, absence like a chance
at life well mulched by dark beds
of silence, better for the brain
to rest a snatched hour before
another dim, short day hauls up again.

A final and yet the first white: the speechless
nougat round which my life
clings with its candy-bitter shell,
having hardened there.

PARTY

March

There must have been a party
to warrant this rose balloon
tied to my wrist.

Pink and plinking, half
aloft demanding
a volley of touches just to stay
up. Yesterday surely—

paper table cloths and cake
crumbing, stereo playlist
marcelled across rolled rugs—

party was? I raise
my hand to ask—the glum sphere
grazes pinkly up the wall.

I usher spoon to mouth
to feed myself—the baggy ball
imposes on my nose.

It takes a craning canter
when he's tuckered—and transfusion
of dignity from a me-part to a he-

part for him still to be
balloony—no mere smear of air
in cheap rubber
cover. We make—

since which
event?—a kind of couple cinched
by wrist and ribbon

taking together the air—
this window cracked
to breeze our cheeks.

These finchy yellow patches
on the kitchen tile where
milk has slopped like beer.
A here and yellow there.

There must have been
a parting where the boom box
and the cocktails left

and guests dug out a snowpath
to boot themselves away.

Balloon and me, puzzle
in which two toys lock,
bob clockily. Sun's
already down again.

As lightness slowly leaves us
and we swim the ruggy static
I recall—the gleaming mop
and almond air of expectation,

the purchased nibbles, sodas,
wines and woofer. The door unlocked
and note about the buzzer.

Then screen goes black
and I—balloon-brain—muzzle
chairleg with my face.

The tin ceiling spreads
as though a sea below. A stamp,
a stomped before. False floor.

Small balloon, you partner mine,
you baby breathing smaller
than a mouse—my kingdom
for a house without confusion!

—orient and corporate
our beings, being
air in some part and in others
matter of a thicker, duller
kind and I am fullblown desperate

to remember—
love—in un-inert un-thingy
drafts of warmth—some gyre to cling
to—rings or rungs to—
bear us up.

[IN A SET OF BOXES]

February

In a set of boxes—my apartment—
I had severed life from

World—the lady
From the trick—split via sword

That should have been mirage
Or else have sent

Soul flying up
To red velvet applause—

But did I ever really cut
Me through?

Was I ever yet mass enough
To conjure into two—

Heft left for each
To give both boxes body,
Soul of their own?

Oh you plush-seated: I was not.
At scene's end
I was split

—Not with mirrors
And trickster hidden chambers
But in truth and no soul

Left behind.
Now my pith is all his own creature
In his sweet meshy box

With the zoo sheets and sea-
Sounds from a speaker.

Better each day at keeping warm
Getting thick like a cobble—

I could not grudge a life
That drums so plummily.

He's sap and a half for charging
The veins of a tree
And spark to spare.

Now my pith is out and not my own.
I move—yes—
Livingbox to diningbox to bedbox.
Apartment above flings hailstones
On the ears—

Someone rushing to their next scene
Choosing shoes choosing lines dropping
Books and wines and parcels
In haste to get away—

Apartment below receives
Us amply: blurred speech tones and grind
Of unpacked bassinet
Snored open on its rusted hinge.

We chandelier their dreaming with our step.

One week in—I wept about the weeks
To wait for clearance of
The full of sex.

Now some weeks post—and prismed
Pluperfect as ice in a tray—

Our shadows fleck
Each clear coffin of intention.

The trapped air gray in frozen water.
Colder than stones
We crackle in our severed grids.

A MOTHER IS A PAPERWEIGHT

February

I press the desk—
wood presses up to me.

Between my heel
and the pinwheeling turf
planet gravity pinches:

paper, folder, plank
and crossplank, floor.

I was mined and heated.
Then I was yours.
I exist because you want

to hold what you know
in just this way.
Document tissue visible, straitened—

like soldiers posed prone after battle
enrolled on a gladed campus,

the fact of weight
picked out in silver nitrate.

You want straight reporting.
The fact that can run
swallowtail or monarch through.
The justice of the well-placed pin.

And yet you give me
pink rosettes, unnecessary polish,
a single eye
open as a baptistry—

You have not smashed me yet.
You still think you need me.

Dear old Newton-lover,
when it seems the large attracts the small
we ignore how the small
exerts its own draw.

I know the earth is enticed toward me—
and also I am not its only.

I know when towered Galileo
released mismatched spheres
earth rushed up to both.
Meeting the odd pair at once.

Nothing has to fall faster
or be greeted belatedly—

ground soars toward us all
interposed in brief
by some delay, the legs—

just so, one idea can surge
toward two minds—
the calculus, the steam engine, writing
light on silver with acid and time, operatic love
or a joke—

with a constant acceleration.

And you
who use me, your bauble
the color of spit
pressing your facts—

eyeing the ceiling, starless
but for what my facets throw up—

see how kinless I am
beached here with my beauty.
Given to holding
order's own sake.

See how lone but kindled.
Lamplight swirling the deepest grooves
where once I was blown—I!

once ardent creature like hot water,
now sentry to the flat end of the facts.

HINGE

January

The door rattles. Blast of pain, and past
the pear-white chill of the birth ward bustles

this odd shadow down my legs and away.
Wet hair styled stiff by the minute's ladle—

you are here and growing to the naked eye new
dizzy space in your lungs. Rigging the topsail

nailsbreadth at a time. Your nails
clear and tiny, row of ellipses erased.

I knew I'd see my insides on your outsides,
how you've been smeared and tossed

like old-time typeset text, like sex. . . .
I knew I'd forgive my body telling all,

as billions had, and also want forgotten
all that spilled ink. Find you neater

genesis than that. A story of a stork—
I see why that's been done before—

the plausible pinch and pinion
when the door swats minutes off like flies,

and off you go for the life you spent hours
clacking backward into.

Like new worlds where height flows
in one direction only, as time does here

on earth, such that once traversed, that perch
can't be chirped upon again. There are places

you can't go back, even if the site remains,
even if the gift of you is storked against

the doorstep where we found you in
the footpath of an otherwise ordinary Tuesday,

day I took piano lessons as a child,
day of learning over and over to loosen

my shoulders so the sound came down
with greater say over *piano* or *forte*, from the whole

body's choice and not just its outer limits.
You are tuned to a pitch that in this dimension

flows just one way, like time, a note that won't
be struck again, belonging to an axis of well-tempered

fingers plucking at the air with bated strings.
Like typeset text you rattle with the news, or knew

at once that setting nowise binds you,
only smears a moment's pigment on a message

changed the more the head line calls for checks
of facts, the more it's recounted and columned,

pressed into held folds, the more

you're here.

A PREGNANT WOMAN IS A SCARECROW

November

It will all end, this particular theater of perpetuum self
unbidden by any mastering hand.
I loved the straw ticking
that filled my chest. I loved the old hogshair adorning my scalp

and the feeling in dirt of my own stakes.
Being free has been its own poem
in a gilt-edged book, a field
shining at its edges around a blurred and glad scotoma.

The corn burns. Gases fix themselves to white hairs
deeper than the workers can see.
They trust the undertaking.
The appetites of soil.

Beyond what I need care for,
faint, near-identical garments are drying on a nylon line.
Should no one stop them
they will soon rock and puff in their lightness.

They torque where they've been clipped.
How happy they look, panting together. Something blue-white
out of Blake. They look like pillow mints
rattling off a bed.

Matter takes its charge from level to level.
I lived this stage as solid,
a boolean of dust. Knowing it's more common
to be liquefied in flow. To pluralize, to *them* myself in others.

I expect that in my after. Unconscionable softness of a planet parting
crust from provisional crust. Baring and effacing
its faults. For the wet flame, the mantle
truer than any hill.

In that astonishing later I will speak into the mouth
of my fellows, which will also be my own
pressed mouth: *Recall. Bevel of one*
creaking limb sloped against starlight. Dry frost.

Mica fleck. Privacy was faienced blue
and lavished like a tomb. But we will not remember.
Lazarettoed in the wet of one rapport
we will not recall it.

STREET CLEANING DAY

November

When I thought myself most honest
I was merely moving
aside from the relevant surface

and not getting down
to the nature of things.

Me in my rattletrap
baring the black road
so the sweeper truck touches
its gray skirts there and departs
with ratty nibbled leaf.

Then I would roll my vehicle back
to the lip of stone fringed above
what's happening in the street.
Little changed.

I mean to announce the coming of a child.
Not a god, not more particular
than all particulars,
but I get lost in simple repetitions
and forget to speak
with my whole heart.

I was what's known
as a *good girl,* completing the exercises,
claws trimmed, a zip on my coat.
O diagnosis!

I see myself now in those forgotten unbeloved
presidents of the nineteenth century
gaunt even when they were fat—

zones of flesh who lied
a bit, bluffed, bought items
not quite for sale, came down
with wintry infections and warred
on small islands.

Who chose a tiny corner
of a big borrowed house as the one place
to slake their muzzles in
foreign stamps, say, or Latin, or theatrical
women.

There is nothing to pity
them for, and yet, watching my white breath
lather and shave
these brick edifices,

I am dumbstruck by all those of us
who evade true grandeur and the crimson
calypso of feeling,

unwrite our own parts
faster than the couriers
can lay sheaves of script at our feet,

slide our phones in and out of pockets—
silvered oars sculling up and down—

as though by dint
of our small motions
the great river would stay down
and be stroked and not enter us.

AGAINST MATERNITY

October

I will not live
like the chipper clump of October hydrangea.
Empty at the center.

Dunes pile
on the garden's granite wall.
Already I feel memory
sapping off my hands.

Dimes on my sockets.
Half mummy, half hot jar of heart.

Who am I if not
vast thirsts—that grasping
at the flexed heel
at the pulse?
Who am I not possessed?

Lathing shapes
undertow my abdomen.
Antimatter world coeval with my own

and stripping through me.
Body thickens but the self
its soleness thins.

A watery heel rises to my belly.
Kerning of stacked and ravenous limbs
hum blank the way the sirens did.

Make me wonder what you are.
Make me questing mad.
Do not keep me

home. Me for sating
whatever need, me adaptable,
me a stock pot for feeding-from,
me home, me numb?

Will it be like silk
on glass—the contrasts
slipping past each other

not knowing how to bite,
to catch—tense past whisked off
snagless?

Will it be like a stroke—block of blank
where tiller was, eyeball
spared but groundless, out

of harness—my soft selfish
and lexical core
sleeping under bracken?

Do not hollow me
Attic and Parthian world.
World of marble and iodine—world with shell
and lapis inlay
flaking from the eyes.

If it had been acceptable
only to move and graze
only to be a thing

you would have taught it.
I would have learned.

Small yellow leaves
press against black asphalt.
Its warmth in the sun
makes them go soft.

They can flatten and settle on the dark.
World that gave me learning and clangor—
Do not make me too grateful. Do not make me too simple.

A.'S DAY

October

It was your birthday yesterday
when one is supposed to think
about time that the fall holds
a meeting with winter and bets
the farm again. Singling out
the middle of the night you
bristling risk arrived in 1985
we hold hands over stingy drinks
in a secretly Midwestern bar
brooding on Atlantic Avenue
like a pink bantam chicken.
A Scorpio's supposed to
be different than me and that's true
sometimes I keep a napkin in my coat
to be ready to make less
of things and handle all
the meals and feelings not to be
foreseen while you, love,
by contrast live naked as Yeats
said he'd agree to but didn't
and the phrases of the moon
write their sea steppes on your ready
hide. You're loyal and
you fling you're like a human
dart you're like a human human,

heart on the gibbous side.
I touch your chin the same
expansive war-chest it took
like a cathedral several generations
to make you, some were dead before
they saw the upper storeys
of your roseate time. It's thin air
that we want, the spires with
their teal and mystic prayers,
and if we're not important then
as fallback to be free. What grows slowly
is the single day, even a birthday, while
the words are way more jumpy
as we wait to find out what
is there for our describing.
We'll have to say the broken fridge,
we'll have to say the warm nights
of ragweed, you'll put a sex scene on it
like the pretty frill on top
of a BLT. True, it's a major
subject but does it belong
everywhere, fine, silly are
the veils on that valiant
erudition and it's hot when
we fuck in our room.

24 WEEKS

Behind this mortal Bone
There knits a bolder One—
—EMILY DICKINSON

September

A Pelvis like a Window.
A smeared Window on a Ferry—public—

well-mapped. A Woman is for everyone.
A wider Gait was wanted:

I walked with Legs pinched tight.
Like Letter—like Clam—

they'll steam the Breach amenable.
An aftertaste of Salt:

eider, piqued, utopian
from Worlds before the Cell.

A Pelvis like a Woman is a public
Clam, a Claim, a Pinkerton Letter.

A Voice asks which Arm
to take some Blood. I had forgotten

the inky Arms! Hung with Veins
near surfacing each day. I say left,

the side of Spleen. Then No, I want
the right. Where Aim and Ire coordinate.

An arm is eider Blanket—inner Barbs
within its Planes of Heat

are piquant, are a public Chapelling
in salt white blue and green.

These thickened Veins do church-work,
make Fools feel they read

by looking at a Window cut in Faces.
Their Eyes move over Slugs of Lead

from Stain to glassy Stain. An Altar
is a Pelvis is a steaming Window Rose

in mullioned Ink. The frank
Meat-Love of all the fake Elect!

You who read off difference
on my Torso's swollen Lectern

happy for a Lemma
of innately sexed Design:

I am more You than Bone-grout
locks your Features

to your Skull. I know and be
more You than all the flaking outcries

settled on your Collar,
your windsored Tie. I comb

your peeling Pate my own.
Bilks and Cozeners,

an Othering is ashen is
a malisoned Presume.

I public on your Pelvis.
I grate the Meat of Roses

on our siamese Spleen. For you
are I ensembled woman-

parted—and I everyone
for You. I ire for

this Body—all ours—
a sinking Ferry mullioned

through the Heart—lowering
between saltwild Signs.

GRANVILLE

Only another head
I have, another heart and breast,
Another music. . . .

—GEORGE HERBERT

July

I was handed an ungrateful soul
and a gewgaw world—
who among us hatched out different,
ecstatically eggtoothed,
without pain?—but this
I know I love and don't deserve
and have: to smell the sulfur
from a country well
rising off your showered arms,
and the citrine hiss at six
of onions in hot butter
snaking up the vents from the rich
and bay-strewn supper-cooking
of our friends below.
The world is working for our good.
The hot lid of day is bluing
and withdrawn. Thrushes finally
cool enough to cry.
In the guest room's preternatural dark,
we could fall chinfirst on this sweetly broken,
bunny-sloping bed
if you'd incline. We could go down

and fix ourselves a sphinx.
Something out of pond-clay
and playing cards to inform me
what the meaning is
in all these morseled rivulets,
merle-blue patches deepening the yard,
robins clocking gospel
in the draft-chinks of the eaves.
Holiness on the head,
perfection on the beasts.
Whatever it is claims
to rise like heat will have to walk
our grubbed, pocked passageways,
collagen and albumin,
fat and iron. College-learning
mineraled and bubbled,
the waterglass left sat.
There is no other way to stir the pot.
To wind our breasts up
painting us aflush.
Whatever it is
claims its little rising
and is listenably dotty
and exact—I thank it
from my carmine hunch

of heart—as though
we'd hulk forever on
just this narthex
built of white
bean and onion,
butter and bread and sex.

EAST OF THE FIRES

June

Under the scaffolds
painted green like flat,

theatrical trees—one pink, wet
nestling on the sidewalk, soft

and scrunched like a quarter-note
rest, soft save

for caliper beak
and talons smaller than rice.

The sky today the color of *that,*
of unidentifiable—maybe robin,

jay, maybe last
of some strain, a week old,

who knows, a tented skin
of froth-milk gray

and clay-urn tones
where muscle bundles

enzyme-tenderize
beneath scant fat.

And I, carrying
a helplessness inside me,

a gruel of growth breathing
smoke from my blood.

The sky today the color of that.
A juvenile flipped

aground, out of one and onto
another larger, harder

broken shell. Thank
God, it wasn't moving.

STILL

June

Tell me about the final day my body—full as it'll go without yet changing
size or shape, denser than it ever packed itself, the last day of Body-Before
—will still not show, when mirror still won't mark how underflesh
has no reserve, no extra give or compress left, the airless torso sedimented on
a pelvic leaded glass, tell me which will be the last time I look at me while
old body's custardy silt still anchors to the barque of how I am.

Say a month. Say tomorrow. Say not now. Was it just now? Won't I know it till it
happened and adrift? Won't I look on non-self me and algebraize its changes?
Is fear-of-future mash note to the past? Oh, shameless how I loved Old Me, prancing,
boozing, flinging my life into crosswalks like salt into boiling water, latching to friends
like a pig-lead brooch. I was a mean sibyl and a sleepy drunk, rocking on the sunup
subway while the girl beside me on the bench curled her lashes with a metal teaspoon,

honest to goodness, rinsed it with a little spit, ate with it a carton of yogurt on
her way to whatever work requires both those sacraments. I, covered
in eyes as hide can be when polished by the mammoth chamois of light rain on
a Friday night. How I envy now those rinses of the slipshod and august. O Old Me,
your morosity at noon, your blackened silver, filthy toenails, doctrines, surmises,
hand between coat buttons like a general astride a chain of sparkling islands!

Have I changed yet outwardly? And is outward only dingy wrapper on the real?
Or does container flavor what it clasps, alter it, the applesauce smell of wrist
under watchband? Like peregrine becoming nearly pet inside its hood. Tell me it's
the last day of Before and I'll go a-mousing, sink my beak beneath the fur of one
last clappered heart. How I feel even now the meat swell under my skin, warm the craw.
Say it's good as here, this change in body's faithless shape. Say it's good. Say still. Say when.

SEVEN WEEKS

May

Only by keeping always one-third full
will my stomach give peace. Empty
it heaves. Topped up, shrieks,
seeks to undo itself.
Is this what I taught it: keep just one shard
of any good thing? Pitch the rest
or moan on emptiness? I think
of each time I was almost falling
in love, crouched a half step behind
the feeling long as I could.
One rye crumb in my throat to soak
how wet the word could make
my tongue. To stopper me.
Little below the breastbone
then but autumn's consommé.
My wrinkled gastric lining
rolling, a rotary phone.
Then giving in so much. Almost always
love fled in a burst. I empty
sat in bilious pain, turned and alone,
a jackknife tossed at a wall, begging
for purchase, drooling down
the particleboard. In part
I've learned. Keep things
at *almost* always. Keep always the give
not quite undone. The half-stopped
seek. The crouch still curled.

The couch with its washable upholstery,
its holsters of grief that afternoon,
in hotel'd midnight, when I misfielded
all the gift for love I almost caught.
Isn't that what heartburn is? Not knowing how
to bed a good thing down? To settle with the good?
To square it where spleen meets rib
I stole in quiet after. Not wreaking me
all across the porcelain. Nothing teaches me
to be full without revolt.
Still I'd almost always steal it all again.

THE FEMININE ENDING IN PROSODY

May

I was walking, then I'd run a few steps farther
not wanting even rhythm's comfort, my forehead's sprouts of skullhair
sweat-thinned, poking, rank as castor

down the urban avenue in the lean summer
shadow of the nursing home's worn manor.

Doubtless someone inside watched, unsure
if I or the television were sobbing, if this were
part of the series whose name was no loss for

forgetting. My heart sagged, over-
ripe, frosted and thawed, slick and heavier
—knowing newly I was pregnant—than whatever
time would settle later.

(Moods like this came harder, faster
than the deep surprise and peace I'd mostly savor, later,
like a baby's first rolling over,
shocked by plan fulfilled at thought's order.)

In this mood's grimmer power,
from the thumb-softened deck of images, all I could muster
was how one particularly nervy, sharp-shinned former lover

—who I thought had reveled in my wolfishness, the blister
on my forefoot where I'd spin away from him or, paw-stretched, canter
back, my hungry pride, my rickety hauteur—

would not have wanted me were I mother.

No matter
the years since, as prudes say, "seeing" each other.
Nor would again forever.
No matter I was loved, had shelter

and no need to beg or hunt, had hung my timber fur
high and away. The glass alembic of my life ashimmer
and melting, its silica in falter,

reshaping—I felt this as loss, poured the hot luster
in whatever iron cast would nurture
a wet and dying thing while it cooled. Render
that in terms of memory: it will linger

on a long-gone curtained afternoon, two bodies facing each other
like stony wed Etruscans on a sepulcher.
Not coupled, or only eye to eye, on the bed's tightened cover

the better to appreciate—do I mean measure—
the rock-honest nakedness of each. As one beast regards another.

And remember when he leaned, light, over
me and murmured
something hard to catch—was it that he was? or
that I was?—a perfect terror, a danger.

2003 SNAPSHOT FOUND IN THE NIGHTSTAND AT MY PARENTS' HOUSE

May

I know the arms—a little plumper than they are now, now that I see myself as seen—
and that they will be carrying something to someone. Always delivering friends
a baked dish, a postcard covered in Proust, some bangle to say I was grateful to be taken up.

The green linen sarong I will wear all that summer—its topmost mash obscuring my belly—
effect classical—I'd hoped—like temples or money. Sixteen, in love for the first
time I could talk about, less furtive, more lavish, than in childhood or now. I am ashamed

to say it now—the boy is worse than ordinary. The soft-sagging garments, loose duffel of face,
cigarettes forever spilling like dried peas from pockets and packs—these things I will take for ease
and age. Were they not on him stray traces of fear, like lint on a coat? Of being measured,

edge and end on view? I nuzzle him. He leans my way, deniably, half accident, half choice.
Perhaps he merely stumbled on my head. He has lived in England one adult year and decided
to speak like the Queen. Mornings, I send allusive notes on where to find the wildflowers I've cut,

tied, and hidden on an outer stump of Roman ruin for him. I watch him in the summer school for clues.
Once or twice he gamely locates the bouquet, takes it somewhere, I don't know. Relieves it
of the sun I hope. Off camera, slumping shocks of campion, yarrow, loosestrife rattle endlessly.

He lectures me on Pound, the hero he'll admit. I watched his chin—so velveteen, so vague
I thought he'd melt. On slippered nerves I softly crawled his face. He often kissed me back. His pension's
padrona, fairy-tale witch, will leave her desk one night a year to sleep. That night he takes me up

the marble stairs. I love the little poppy on the sheet. He hustles me downstairs, the screaming padrona . . .
End of play. Plumped up like a heap of bedding on the stammering pullman bus,
my visiting mother beside me, we'll lumber out to Cervignano. Then the train to Venice. Bus scrapes

beside a crammed tabaccheria and I make as if to miss, fathoms below on the sidewalk, his dark form
like a trout. He rifles too quickly through some photos of his own. The lido and the portals of winged lions
and my green skirt. Hunger will round on me like a cup—so gentle-walled I hardly know

I'm trapped. Edgeless, it is all edge. Fogged and indefinite, it is forever. It is not the boy I feel a sudden
anger toward. But what I know will happen next to this girl's arms. How soon giving will perplex me.
I will knock around yet with my fat ladings, trinkets, potlatch, relics, little notes. But will mortify

this bent I have for fetching like a dog. And warp against it, steel myself alone.
And even when alive with gift, feel at pains to pass it off as chores, as love of work. Not love of love.
Not the iris's opalled opening, its black and tipping basket wide for more and more retinal light.

Occasionally I confuse me with the photographic girl I was. I slide my face into the plastic sleeve.
What appetite can activate me now? A flash smacks in dusk against my gaze. The eyeball, charged
with hidden blood, reflects a hungry, ruby disc on film, the red-eye error common in the amateur portrait.

ADDENDUM

May

What exes made plain—
in recollection if not in
actual thumbswirls on
edges of mirror, handles
of fridge, carpals, travel
visas, iPhones, high sec

clearances, my lips,
everything that requires
touch but blemishes
when so anointed, given
the natural acids and oils
we, helpless, grace or grease
our company with, mazed
singular in whorls once thought
irreproducible, now known

better—was pressure's
accomplishment, force
over area, how bad I wanted
to beg and be begged
for love, how rocks melt
down with it, fine
containment, the once-
in-an-ice-age (so seems it,
in it) gnash, and how
the might of circum-

scribed restriction
made contents glow, just

as there's no uglier,
more watchable sight than
mallow of volcano rubbing
its slow sludge-edge
along the land, belching,
crimson-bottomed, crisping
black at its top, I've never
been able to turn off

the video, I just want
to see what force can do
re-formed as heat, eat
hill, eat vale—and I do
believe a marriage can
have this hunger and color

but with effort of
a different kind, not the plates
making new land out
of freshest hot release,
not so strange—a ridge
consistently sunned, perhaps—
a place that takes a daily

light. Something in the state
of pregnancy made each life-
edge stand out brighter,
chapter by old chapter
selvaged, thick, more keen
the recall—what each

desire had meant and through
what small channel of
planet's opportunity had
stone flung up in waves.
Do you ever get
the feeling there is air
in what you took
for rock? That nations
have been moving
in inches? In liquid
dust? The past,

its dumb dalliances
or great seriousness-es,
spits from its red core
charred encounters, silicate
chains of seismic fire—
blossoms brief next to life

as it is now—its false air
of never ending and of being

all I know. I knew, I know
this gravid obsession
with loves I've had, turning
exes and not-evens over
in mind is, was, chemical
and also real, forgivable

and also suffer-strewing—
something I will look
back and Polynesia-red
blush for, not having
been able to help myself
replaying the clips

of magnificent disaster
of the whole face
citrine-lit and then shorn
off in smoke and the new
face that comes, that came,
out of those splits
afloat the world.

A PREGNANT WOMAN IS A COMET

April

I am dark, dark—
then scraped against the planet's windbreak

lit. Then black again
dense hovel of
ice I am.

Do not draw me
to the unstark earth's beds and hedges.

I see what that would be—
too many different tans and browns.
The uncommitted.

The chromatics,
the *this* rubbed into *that.*

Of course I dream.
Earth's north shoulder once,
a coast. Trees and—
a mile off—the waxy sea.

And the sly submission
in that landscape—among the oaks,
a gradual untangling
to the meek dwarves of the coast.

Needlepoint light. Each tablecloth
of grass so proud
to please the forefoot.

Then the water
with its salt in sheaved
titrations. Passing like cider

to brandy to the vanishing
rub on a fevered chest.
Everything done in sane and useful steps.

I will not be moderated.

I see what training does
and the round tides—
a marsh like a woman
selling fine things
on a hanging scale.

Stillness of good measure,
waitfulness in the swiveling torso.
Picking up and setting down.

It was a nightmare, such gentleness.

Understand I've shed
pretense to glow.

My dust burns then doesn't.
There is no shade.

You think your subtlety acquits you?

I see people running
fingers over tuning knobs,
lens cases, drawing my likeness
onto a glass field.

As though they could handle
better my reduction.

Some man compares
my rampant stone
to hair in the strokingest voice.

At his feet a cat swirls
its tabby back.
Indefinite and owned.

And then I wake.
Forget it, I pitch myself
to the unlit fast.

YOU

April

Clench, cramp, implode, spring, relax, make two from one: I see you cells
pinch yourselves raw on a dim filmstrip adhered to my mind, making the thing

in the middle-school screen, like one Christmas light torn off a strand, or a corner
of bubble wrap clung to a shipped jar, you rage under the microscope's light,

you puff and suck, the paroxysm of another doubling, but still pushed up
against yourself, somehow you know to be cliquey and gummy, another cresting

corner of you already beginning the next swell. Inside me you rail on in secret, eyeless
ambush, you let out the hem of another armada and soon you will learn to drink

down blood. Six weeks in forty. Want and fear, oldest orifices, grip me, chafe me, tongue
at my timeshare, dissolve the document to salivary pulp, all the bylaws that ringed me,

the riders I rode. This motor thrashing fingerbreadth beneath the hull, its movements
not mine, these paces, rates, chyron-crawls, and inner increments, these inclines,

beckonings, siphons, indentures, a world of increase without my mind's direction,
my rapping baton, my wish to keep you but slow you, steer you, pause you on a skate-toe's

rubber brake, lay you on ice and look at you a while, cool you in a jeweler's velvet drawer,
write a few lines today, keep the key for you in an old wool coat, find you later

with a twenty-dollar bill, take you out my marble cache, my mammon, grow you out
some more like schoolgirl bangs, make the built world halt, be I, be paddling down

an empty pond in an empty body, alone. I was pumice once, I floated and scratched,
I slew towns with the juices of the planet's mantle, I was practically male, I brittled

when the magma cooled and left limbs where they slept. Will you let me gallop lava again
on Naples and Martinique, will you turn a proto-eye-place to my prowls, predations,

my mercury harebrains, my mouth, my me, my taking my time, my take, my taking?
Will you wait until I bid you forth? I who never ask before seizing. You who know nothing

of juddering between delay, delicious, and bone and meat that say what shambles say,
that time is the knife and gneiss and not the ice chest. Will you keep you. You who know

nothing yet.

SIMPLE

April

My heart is completely simple, of one
substance like a mole, a dark heap

of pigment mired in a bland
it doesn't mind. My mouth

is a promise in a driver's side mirror
and adjusts with a button that gives

with a pinky-flick. My feet demurely
callused because I will work and work.

I may as well have had just one organ,
so simple am I, one tube like a sea sponge

with brine washing my osculum,
crumbing up my fibrous pores. There is nothing

scary, amiss, or unrelatable about me,
who am *comme il faut*. You'd think

I was a plant, you'd think *no problem!*
getting closer. Nothing to see at all, folks,

though no impediment to linger
should you choose. What the bleached coral

don't say: how they drank today's hot chalice
all themselves. No one put me up to sipping

risk and sitting pretty. What the reefs
don't tell twirls deep in their two-dozen

thousand fevered genes, similar in number
to the human, though sickened by the sun blocks,

the way you like your skin to take the light
without absorbing one thing. The things

you hear down here. Even the lowing whales
replicating every sunken liner's final strut,

I let them go on, I am after bigger psychic fish,
I stand before Sancta Simplicitas and let her twitch

my veil and burn my books. I love an idol
who permits a dish of meat at each foot,

the dark flesh and the light, the spectrum
of the hunt. I love a good Doppler effect, am game

to the sluicing vowels and half-heard yodels
moving beyond my sessile place. But you who take

redshift to excess, always eluding, evading,
evaporating, why so wary? You, rounding

a corner like a double glassed bodega when I
would have settled for heartfelt credit.

I have tried labor and I have tried play. I looked
into a tiny compact and saw the big face

and the tiny sponge. I, prey for dregs
of attention, four drags on a light that's good

I know for a dozen. When I take up your day
and suck it down like a bag tight with helium,

daffy and lung-light, I am not sustained.
I am dying from taking. My gullet

capers like a piccolo. If I could have the whole
of you, the denser thing, pie-weight

and plumb-line, the vital pith, I think it would
enough me for beyond. You'd hardly notice.

I'd give you back, I promise, to yourself.

KEEPING HOUSE

March

Hard to square how much I wanted
with how much requested:

the ask and the take
like two inscribed columns against

a pink dawning margin, or the classic
rabbit-duck illusion hinging

on the aimless eye.
I was proper, merciful—

I wanted the warfarined mouse on the rug
to be sleeping only.

I watched the train flow by
and never once took it.

I was becoming a woman
like the dead:

fond of coins, dreams, cakes,
votives, hopeless

at adding to my deeds.
For a week I tried keeping

forks and spoons in separate
drawered slots. But everything

that aids you tends
toward a similar handle.

You accustom to a certain
blue enamel, to a few blue

inches between you
and the slop.

When I flushed away
my pills to make a baby

cross the red carpet
and tootle at the planetary flash

a recreant hunger rattled me.
I sat open-legged

at my husband's feet
like a splayed magazine

and waited, paludal, for one
of the two ways of keeping book,

the rabbit, or the duck
—do you see

the long haul
as velveteen or bill?

Of "housekeeping" and "keeping house,"
which title tells you more

of how I did?
Any way

I looked, the neighbor's dog downstairs
had a tumor behind

one eye standing
out poached and disabused.

The dryer in the basement
so stuffed along its hose with skin and thread

we wore our fellow tenants
like a beard.

The baby wore a trench and specs,
slipped back into the crowd.

As banister and vinyl
siding came undone, so too

my pretense to scholarship,
my hours at the institutes for tick and tock.

So-and-so's drone, mike angled
like a rotting corsage,

it all seemed a tale absent
the frazzle of seduction,

Scheherazade at the fish counter
too behaved with the numbered

white tongue of her turn.
Waiting for the sign to match her slip.

One can wait to be swept up
for weeks and weeks.

Rattling in my carrel, how I wanted out
to my yellow-sided house,

my Decadent Movement.
Malady of dreaming!

The basement with its gallery of paint cans,
the washer-dryer leashed

to ghosts and fumes.
The "good eye" rufous, desperately twinkling,

its confrere blind and bulging
like a belly. Years after, dog and banister

put or taken down,
I still have my domestic arts.

I rent and rend and rut.
I think I think of certain animals

as the signs for certain years
because there is no actual heir to flesh.

Rabbit, duck, or dogfish,
any eye could be the volta.

Nights when the train veered by,
almost and never reaching us,

I licked my cornered parts
the way a dog would

or a duck parting its plumage to unearth
its secret fur-white coney pelt, having

always favored the open gloss
over being over it.

MINUS TIME

March, and the infinite Before

Now you have no matter to you. Not even one cell and you
cannot be studied or moved. You cannot even be loved or made

from love or badly because you are not yet in this yawning time
before you, but can be talked to, as I talk sometimes to Wallace Stevens

or my mother's mother, touching the flavor of their definite
articles to my collar line—you un-here, but address adheres,

a massless sticky golden resin of pre- and post-presence
with rosy and amber sillage, the ghost's light pollution

of the human district outside the skidding limits of the pulsatile
beyond which our pulseless unbirth stretches one way,

and then our death. Two ungridded sprawls. All around
and outside that picayune but urbane zone where your life will go,

you are dispossessed of life but visible, almost, with the right
belief and sulfur pended in the eastern air just when the sun slings up.

The robins occupied today and you have none of it, like Sappho
in 1848, you too simply were not there, and this may cause you

envy or the regret of one who syncopates against the turnstile
and misses the advertised bus. Why we do not abhor our pre-life,

as infinitely long and thoughtless as our death—maybe it *is*
our death, mirrored: not mystic but math, my mind

likely as absent in 1789 as 2089, the gristle in my knuckles
uncapped and eking out some other work, the same carbon actors,

a different season at the rep—the problem speaks First
Gentleman's line but can't explain the minor chord swelling from

the pit. And so having you, meaning delivering you—two idioms
at odds to say, for me, there is a hoarding side to this and another

that is indigent and mendicant forever—and even more so conceiving
the start of you, these events will make one holler at death

whom one sees right there chilled in the subzero of the *x* axis, walled off
for now by the present tense, like the peeping Tom at my window

once in Virginia—I couldn't meet his eyes for fear of what they'd show
me but described over and over to the cop his white sneakers.

The linty, graying tongue flung sidelong like smoke in a child's
picture of the dream home's chimney. Yeah kid. Now I wouldn't

make that call but I know that pile of missed centuries is out there
still by the dog gate and the compost, and that loving to look

is the most common cause of grief in America. "One" can be a high-
falutin' "I" or "you," but here you are not a one yet, and the heathered purple

nullity of sleep drapes the cosmic static that can hold your pronouns
in the prop room until that season arrives. When you begin

to grow it will become apparent that need and desire are
the primary colors of the living—normal, appetitive, endless

until death—and so I try to pat the cheek of all my ogreish covets,
as they are just the larger polymers of all the monomers grasping

and blocking and shredding, right down to blood and bone.
For nine months pregnant plus ten months nursing I will feel

my body as prison and will file tunnels toward any signal
of outpost past the boundaries. I will fear that as a baby grows,

a mother shrinks, dilutes in milk and water until she's no more
there than any grain of salt vanished in the bath. I will want:

to be famous, to get fucked, to rehome the dog, to document,
to trip, to drink till blackout, to emigrate, to diarize, to divorce,

to crash diet, to flip the car, to chronicle, to lip-fill, to kill my plants,
to collect, to tattoo, to rekindle, to die, to disappear. This does not

concern you except as you may also one day feel in life a tin-pot
trammeling that fills your head with oily rags on fire. May it not.

Not ever. Here now in the quiet of being-not, sweet no-one soon beloved,
you non-exist in lush subjunctive I can picture as a futon made of

asteroidal plush, the kind of halfway furniture designed for those
in-between years when soon-humans lie on their backs with their fellows

and their snacks and think on the hard stop we spring from,
long-odded, impossible and here. A wail goes up from the phantoms

of all future desires—they too are dorming here in the infinite Before,
and rattle on the hot plate in the twitchy angles that will

one day have mass and muscle and thirst of their own. Here I saw
a new heaven and a new earth, glassed in breathy readiness

like a warm terrarium under its halogens, and around it
the tarry gulf of all time and all other concatenations

of possible events, garbage-patch lapping at the shoreline,
the collar of the real. And I knew the bright light I focused on

would wash up on that shore, or another would, or another,
and that this would be my life's unfolding next: delivering you

(the black gulf did), meaning having you (in the sense of that
expulsion), meaning conceiving enough of the subjunctive mood

to be standing there, loving to look, at the sprawl of all eras
some part of which you will one day touch without me, you reaching

that district and desiring whatever you desire with a spotlight
trained on the eggs of that to incubate their bursting novas.

NOTES

"Three and a Dog": "And they lived in a warm wooden tree" quotes Margaret Wise Brown's *Little Fur Family.* The Sophie Calle/Greg Shephard movie referenced is *Double Blind* (alternate title *No Sex Last Night*).

"In Flower" takes its title from the second volume of Marcel Proust's *In Search of Lost Time.*

"Writing and Nursing" references advice given in Marcella Hazan's *Essentials of Classic Italian Cooking* and in Madhur Jaffrey's *Vegetarian India: A Journey Through the Best of Indian Home Cooking.*

"March 20, 2023": The exploration of shades of white is indebted to *Cataract*, by John Berger with illustrations by Selçuk Demirel.

"24 Weeks": The Emily Dickinson poem cited is "No Rack can torture me" (384).

"Granville": The epigraph and italicized lines are from George Herbert's "Aaron" (with Herbert's "breast" transformed into "beasts").

"Keeping House": The phrase "malady of dreaming" comes from Oscar Wilde's *The Picture of Dorian Gray*, describing the insalubrious effect of Dorian's yellow notebook.

"Minus Time" makes use of Revelation 21:1.

ACKNOWLEDGMENTS

Some of these poems first appeared in *Alaska Quarterly Review* ("Granville"), *The Atlantic* ("Hinge"), *Conjunctions* ("Writing and Nursing," "24 Weeks," "Teaching Speech," "First Cut"), *Harper's* ("Keeping House"), *House House Magazine* ("Playoffs"), *LARB Quarterly* ("You"), *n+1* ("Three and a Dog," "March 20, 2023"), *The New York Review of Books* ("Still"), *The New Yorker* ("Seven Weeks," "Pregnancy on Street Cleaning Day," "Simple"), and *The Yale Review* ("The Scarecrow"). "A.'s Day" and "Film Maudit" first appeared in the chapbook *Keeping House: Six Longer Love Poems* (Center for Book Arts). Thanks to the editors and staff who took excellent care of them.

Thanks to MacDowell, the James Merrill House, and Millay Arts for providing time, space, kindness, and material support for writing and revision.

Thanks to many friends and colleagues, too numerous to list in full, for their love and insights, poetic and otherwise. For their unstinting care work, thanks to Lee Kolbe, Brenda Locher, and all the wonderful others in my families of origin and marriage; Aizada Sagynbekova, Shaknoza Nozirova, and Anzia Anderson; and every teacher at Tiny Steps and PKA. Several friends have been truly formidable biathletes in looking after and appreciating both my writing and my child, especially Stephanie Bernhard, Jo Biggs, Sonia Feigelson, and Gwen Harper. Adrienne Raphel and David Wallace have also been painstaking early readers. For strokes of brilliant and generous co-parenting, thanks to Atossa Abrahamian, Halle Butler, Meechal Hoffman, Claire Lehmann, Mojo Lorwin, Sarah Lustbader, Laurence Marie, Daniel May, Sam Sacks, Christine Smallwood, Anna Sussman, all of "Leora's reading group," and many more.

Thanks to Rachel Lindheim in particular for her curiosity, wisdom, and provocation, without which this manuscript would not be.

Thanks, most of all, to Andrew and Sandro for every day in your company.